50 Snacks for Movie Night

By: Kelly Johnson

Table of Contents

- Popcorn with Butter and Salt
- Nachos with Cheese
- Cheese and Cracker Platter
- Veggie Platter with Hummus
- Mini Pizzas
- Sweet and Salty Trail Mix
- Chocolate-Covered Pretzels
- Mozzarella Sticks
- Baked Potato Skins
- Soft Pretzels with Mustard
- Veggie Spring Rolls
- Guacamole and Chips
- Buffalo Chicken Dip
- Pigs in a Blanket
- Mini Tacos
- Fruit Skewers
- Cheese Quesadillas
- Popcorn with Caramel
- S'mores Bites
- Spicy Roasted Chickpeas
- Chicken Wings
- Cinnamon Sugar Pretzels
- Veggie Chips
- Jalapeño Poppers
- Roasted Almonds
- Mini Sandwiches
- Potato Wedges with Ketchup
- Baked Zucchini Fries
- Chocolate Fudge Brownies
- Cheese-Stuffed Mushrooms
- Rice Cake Crisps
- Chips and Salsa
- Frozen Grapes
- Mini Burgers
- Chocolate-Covered Almonds

- Antipasto Skewers
- Spinach and Artichoke Dip
- Mini Quiches
- Caramel Popcorn
- Dried Fruit Mix
- Onion Rings
- Popcorn Chicken
- Parmesan Crisps
- Chocolate-Covered Strawberries
- Sausage Rolls
- Veggie and Cheese Kabobs
- Cinnamon Apple Chips
- Baked Brie with Crackers
- Puffed Rice Bars
- Mini Pancakes with Syrup

Popcorn with Butter and Salt

Ingredients:

- 1/2 cup popcorn kernels
- 2 tablespoons butter
- Salt to taste

Instructions:

1. **Pop the popcorn:** Heat a large pot over medium heat. Add the popcorn kernels and cover with a lid. Shake the pot occasionally until the popping slows down. Remove from heat.
2. **Butter the popcorn:** Melt the butter in a small saucepan or microwave.
3. **Season:** Drizzle the melted butter over the popcorn and toss to coat. Sprinkle with salt to taste.
4. **Serve:** Enjoy immediately.

Nachos with Cheese

Ingredients:

- 1 bag tortilla chips
- 2 cups shredded cheddar cheese
- 1/2 cup jalapeños, sliced (optional)
- Sour cream, salsa, and guacamole for serving

Instructions:

1. **Prepare the nachos:** Preheat the oven to 375°F (190°C). Spread the tortilla chips evenly on a baking sheet.
2. **Add cheese and toppings:** Sprinkle the shredded cheddar cheese evenly over the chips. Add sliced jalapeños if desired.
3. **Bake:** Bake for 5-7 minutes, or until the cheese is melted and bubbly.
4. **Serve:** Serve with sour cream, salsa, and guacamole.

Cheese and Cracker Platter

Ingredients:

- 1 block of cheddar cheese, sliced
- 1 block of brie cheese, sliced
- 1 box of assorted crackers (e.g., water crackers, wheat crackers, or flavored crackers)
- Grapes, apples, or figs for garnish (optional)

Instructions:

1. **Arrange the platter:** On a large platter, arrange the sliced cheeses and crackers.
2. **Add garnish:** Add fruits like grapes, apple slices, or figs for a fresh touch.
3. **Serve:** Serve as an appetizer or snack.

Veggie Platter with Hummus

Ingredients:

- 1 cucumber, sliced
- 1 cup baby carrots
- 1 bell pepper, sliced
- 1 cup cherry tomatoes
- 1/2 cup celery, sliced
- 1 cup hummus for dipping

Instructions:

1. **Prepare the vegetables:** Wash and slice the vegetables into bite-sized pieces.
2. **Arrange the platter:** On a large platter, arrange the sliced vegetables in a circle or random pattern.
3. **Serve:** Serve with a bowl of hummus in the center for dipping.

Mini Pizzas

Ingredients:

- 4 mini pizza crusts (store-bought or homemade)
- 1/2 cup pizza sauce
- 1 cup shredded mozzarella cheese
- 1/4 cup pepperoni slices or your favorite toppings

Instructions:

1. **Preheat the oven:** Preheat to 400°F (200°C).
2. **Assemble the pizzas:** Spread pizza sauce on each mini crust. Top with mozzarella cheese and your desired toppings.
3. **Bake:** Bake for 8-10 minutes, or until the cheese is melted and bubbly.
4. **Serve:** Remove from the oven and let cool slightly before serving.

Sweet and Salty Trail Mix

Ingredients:

- 1 cup pretzels
- 1/2 cup salted almonds
- 1/2 cup chocolate chips
- 1/2 cup dried cranberries
- 1/2 cup sunflower seeds

Instructions:

1. **Combine ingredients:** In a large bowl, mix together the pretzels, almonds, chocolate chips, dried cranberries, and sunflower seeds.
2. **Serve:** Serve immediately or store in an airtight container.

Chocolate-Covered Pretzels

Ingredients:

- 1 bag mini pretzels
- 1 cup chocolate chips (dark, milk, or white)
- Sprinkles or sea salt (optional)

Instructions:

1. **Melt the chocolate:** In a microwave-safe bowl, melt the chocolate chips in 30-second intervals, stirring in between, until smooth.
2. **Dip the pretzels:** Dip each pretzel into the melted chocolate, covering about half of it. Let the excess chocolate drip off.
3. **Set and garnish:** Place the dipped pretzels on a baking sheet lined with parchment paper. Sprinkle with sea salt or sprinkles if desired. Let them cool and harden.
4. **Serve:** Once set, enjoy or store in an airtight container.

Mozzarella Sticks

Ingredients:

- 12 mozzarella cheese sticks
- 1/2 cup flour
- 2 eggs, beaten
- 1 cup breadcrumbs (preferably seasoned)
- 1/2 cup marinara sauce for dipping
- Vegetable oil for frying

Instructions:

1. **Prepare the breading:** Set up a breading station with flour in one bowl, beaten eggs in another, and breadcrumbs in a third.
2. **Bread the cheese sticks:** Dip each mozzarella stick into the flour, then the egg, and coat with breadcrumbs. Repeat for all cheese sticks.
3. **Fry the sticks:** Heat vegetable oil in a deep pan over medium heat. Fry the cheese sticks for 2-3 minutes, or until golden and crispy.
4. **Serve:** Drain on paper towels and serve with marinara sauce for dipping.

Baked Potato Skins

Ingredients:

- 4 large russet potatoes
- 2 tablespoons olive oil
- 1 cup shredded cheddar cheese
- 1/2 cup sour cream
- 4 slices bacon, cooked and crumbled
- 2 tablespoons chopped green onions

Instructions:

1. **Bake the potatoes:** Preheat the oven to 400°F (200°C). Prick the potatoes with a fork and bake them for 45-60 minutes until tender.
2. **Prepare the skins:** Let the potatoes cool slightly. Cut them in half and scoop out the insides, leaving a thin layer of potato.
3. **Bake the skins:** Brush the skins with olive oil and bake for an additional 10-15 minutes until crispy.
4. **Fill the skins:** Top with shredded cheese, crumbled bacon, and bake for another 5 minutes until the cheese melts.
5. **Serve:** Serve with sour cream and green onions on top.

Soft Pretzels with Mustard

Ingredients:

- 1 package soft pretzel dough (store-bought or homemade)
- Coarse salt
- Mustard for dipping

Instructions:

1. **Prepare the dough:** If using store-bought dough, follow the package instructions. For homemade dough, roll out individual pretzels.
2. **Boil the pretzels:** Bring a pot of water to a boil, and add 1 tablespoon of baking soda. Boil each pretzel for 30 seconds before removing and placing them on a baking sheet.
3. **Bake:** Sprinkle the pretzels with coarse salt and bake at 375°F (190°C) for 12-15 minutes, or until golden brown.
4. **Serve:** Serve warm with mustard for dipping.

Veggie Spring Rolls

Ingredients:

- 8 rice paper wrappers
- 1 cup shredded lettuce
- 1/2 cup shredded carrots
- 1 cucumber, julienned
- 1/2 bell pepper, julienned
- Fresh cilantro leaves
- 1/4 cup rice noodles (optional)
- 1/4 cup hoisin sauce or peanut sauce for dipping

Instructions:

1. **Prepare the vegetables:** Wash and cut all the vegetables into thin strips.
2. **Soften the rice papers:** Dip each rice paper wrapper into warm water for about 10-15 seconds, until soft. Lay it flat on a clean surface.
3. **Assemble the rolls:** Place a small amount of shredded lettuce, carrots, cucumber, bell pepper, cilantro, and rice noodles (if using) in the center of the rice paper.
4. **Roll the spring rolls:** Fold the sides of the rice paper over the filling and roll tightly. Repeat with remaining wrappers.
5. **Serve:** Serve immediately with hoisin or peanut dipping sauce.

Guacamole and Chips

Ingredients:

- 3 ripe avocados, peeled and mashed
- 1/2 onion, finely chopped
- 1 tomato, diced
- 1 tablespoon lime juice
- 1/4 cup cilantro, chopped
- Salt and pepper to taste
- Tortilla chips for dipping

Instructions:

1. **Mash the avocados:** In a bowl, mash the avocados with a fork or potato masher until smooth but still chunky.
2. **Add the ingredients:** Stir in the chopped onion, tomato, cilantro, and lime juice. Season with salt and pepper.
3. **Serve:** Serve the guacamole with tortilla chips.

Buffalo Chicken Dip

Ingredients:

- 2 cups cooked chicken, shredded
- 8 oz cream cheese, softened
- 1/2 cup ranch dressing
- 1/2 cup buffalo wing sauce
- 1 1/2 cups shredded cheddar cheese

Instructions:

1. **Preheat the oven:** Preheat the oven to 350°F (175°C).
2. **Mix the ingredients:** In a mixing bowl, combine the shredded chicken, cream cheese, ranch dressing, buffalo sauce, and 1 cup of shredded cheddar cheese.
3. **Bake:** Transfer the mixture to a baking dish and top with the remaining 1/2 cup of shredded cheddar cheese. Bake for 20-25 minutes or until bubbly and golden.
4. **Serve:** Serve with tortilla chips, crackers, or celery sticks.

Pigs in a Blanket

Ingredients:

- 1 package mini cocktail sausages
- 1 package crescent roll dough
- 1 tablespoon mustard or ketchup (optional)

Instructions:

1. **Preheat the oven:** Preheat the oven to 375°F (190°C).
2. **Prepare the dough:** Unroll the crescent roll dough and cut into small triangles.
3. **Wrap the sausages:** Place a mini sausage on the wide end of each triangle and roll them up.
4. **Bake:** Place the rolled-up sausages on a baking sheet and bake for 10-12 minutes, or until golden brown.
5. **Serve:** Serve warm with mustard or ketchup for dipping.

Mini Tacos

Ingredients:

- 1 package mini taco shells or tortillas
- 1 lb ground beef or chicken, cooked
- 1 packet taco seasoning
- 1 cup shredded cheddar cheese
- 1/2 cup sour cream
- Salsa and guacamole for serving

Instructions:

1. **Prepare the filling:** Cook the ground beef or chicken in a skillet, adding the taco seasoning and following the package instructions.
2. **Fill the tacos:** Spoon the taco filling into each mini taco shell. Top with shredded cheddar cheese.
3. **Serve:** Serve with sour cream, salsa, and guacamole.

Fruit Skewers

Ingredients:

- 1 cup strawberries, hulled
- 1 cup pineapple chunks
- 1 banana, sliced
- 1 cup grapes
- Wooden skewers

Instructions:

1. **Prepare the fruit:** Wash and cut the fruit into bite-sized pieces.
2. **Assemble the skewers:** Thread the fruit pieces onto the wooden skewers, alternating between different fruits.
3. **Serve:** Serve the fruit skewers chilled or at room temperature.

Cheese Quesadillas

Ingredients:

- 4 flour tortillas
- 2 cups shredded cheddar cheese
- 1/2 cup shredded mozzarella cheese
- 2 tablespoons butter

Instructions:

1. **Prepare the quesadillas:** Heat a skillet over medium heat. Place one tortilla in the skillet and sprinkle with a mixture of cheddar and mozzarella cheese.
2. **Cook:** Place another tortilla on top and cook for 2-3 minutes on each side, or until golden brown and the cheese is melted.
3. **Serve:** Cut into wedges and serve with salsa, sour cream, or guacamole.

Popcorn with Caramel

Ingredients:

- 1/2 cup popcorn kernels
- 1 cup unsalted butter
- 1 cup brown sugar
- 1/2 cup corn syrup
- 1/2 teaspoon baking soda
- 1/2 teaspoon vanilla extract

Instructions:

1. **Pop the popcorn:** Pop the popcorn kernels and set aside.
2. **Make the caramel sauce:** In a saucepan, melt the butter over medium heat. Add the brown sugar and corn syrup and stir to combine. Bring to a boil and cook for 4-5 minutes, stirring occasionally.
3. **Add baking soda and vanilla:** Remove from heat and stir in the baking soda and vanilla extract.
4. **Coat the popcorn:** Pour the caramel sauce over the popped popcorn and toss to coat evenly.
5. **Cool and serve:** Let the caramel popcorn cool before serving.

S'mores Bites

Ingredients:

- 1 package graham crackers
- 1 cup mini marshmallows
- 1/2 cup chocolate chips
- 1/4 cup butter, melted

Instructions:

1. **Prepare the graham crackers:** Break the graham crackers into small squares.
2. **Assemble the bites:** Place a mini marshmallow and a few chocolate chips on top of each graham cracker square.
3. **Melt the chocolate:** Melt the chocolate chips and drizzle over the marshmallows and graham crackers.
4. **Serve:** Let the chocolate harden before serving.

Spicy Roasted Chickpeas

Ingredients:

- 2 cans chickpeas, drained and rinsed
- 2 tablespoons olive oil
- 1 teaspoon smoked paprika
- 1/2 teaspoon ground cumin
- 1/2 teaspoon garlic powder
- 1/4 teaspoon cayenne pepper
- Salt to taste

Instructions:

1. **Preheat the oven:** Preheat the oven to 400°F (200°C).
2. **Prepare the chickpeas:** Pat the chickpeas dry with a paper towel to remove excess moisture.
3. **Season:** Toss the chickpeas in olive oil, paprika, cumin, garlic powder, cayenne, and salt until evenly coated.
4. **Roast:** Spread the chickpeas on a baking sheet in a single layer. Roast for 30-40 minutes, shaking the pan halfway through.
5. **Serve:** Once crispy, remove from the oven and let cool before serving.

Chicken Wings

Ingredients:

- 12 chicken wings, separated into drumettes and flats
- 2 tablespoons olive oil
- 1 tablespoon garlic powder
- 1 tablespoon onion powder
- 1 teaspoon paprika
- 1/2 teaspoon salt
- 1/2 teaspoon black pepper
- 1/2 cup buffalo sauce (optional)

Instructions:

1. **Preheat the oven:** Preheat the oven to 400°F (200°C).
2. **Season the wings:** Toss the chicken wings in olive oil, garlic powder, onion powder, paprika, salt, and pepper until evenly coated.
3. **Roast:** Arrange the wings in a single layer on a baking sheet and bake for 25-30 minutes, flipping halfway through.
4. **Optional buffalo sauce:** If using, toss the baked wings in buffalo sauce before serving.
5. **Serve:** Serve with ranch or blue cheese dipping sauce.

Cinnamon Sugar Pretzels

Ingredients:

- 1 package pretzel bites or pretzel rods
- 1/4 cup unsalted butter, melted
- 1/4 cup sugar
- 1 tablespoon cinnamon

Instructions:

1. **Preheat the oven:** Preheat the oven to 350°F (175°C).
2. **Prepare the pretzels:** Lay the pretzel bites or rods on a baking sheet.
3. **Mix the cinnamon sugar:** In a small bowl, combine the sugar and cinnamon.
4. **Coat the pretzels:** Brush the melted butter over the pretzels and sprinkle generously with the cinnamon sugar mixture.
5. **Bake:** Bake for 8-10 minutes until golden brown and aromatic.
6. **Serve:** Let cool slightly before serving.

Veggie Chips

Ingredients:

- 2 cups mixed root vegetables (sweet potatoes, beets, carrots), thinly sliced
- 2 tablespoons olive oil
- 1 teaspoon sea salt
- 1/2 teaspoon black pepper
- 1/2 teaspoon paprika (optional)

Instructions:

1. **Preheat the oven:** Preheat the oven to 400°F (200°C).
2. **Prepare the vegetables:** Slice the root vegetables thinly using a mandolin or sharp knife.
3. **Season:** Toss the vegetables in olive oil, salt, pepper, and paprika.
4. **Bake:** Spread the slices on a baking sheet in a single layer and bake for 20-25 minutes, flipping halfway through.
5. **Serve:** Let cool before serving.

Jalapeño Poppers

Ingredients:

- 10 fresh jalapeños, halved and seeded
- 8 oz cream cheese, softened
- 1/2 cup shredded cheddar cheese
- 1/2 teaspoon garlic powder
- 1/4 teaspoon smoked paprika
- 1/4 cup panko breadcrumbs
- 1 tablespoon olive oil

Instructions:

1. **Preheat the oven:** Preheat the oven to 375°F (190°C).
2. **Prepare the jalapeños:** Cut the jalapeños in half lengthwise and remove the seeds.
3. **Make the filling:** Mix cream cheese, cheddar cheese, garlic powder, and smoked paprika in a bowl.
4. **Fill the jalapeños:** Stuff each jalapeño half with the cheese mixture.
5. **Top with breadcrumbs:** Sprinkle the filled jalapeños with panko breadcrumbs and drizzle with olive oil.
6. **Bake:** Place on a baking sheet and bake for 20-25 minutes until golden and bubbly.
7. **Serve:** Let cool slightly before serving.

Roasted Almonds

Ingredients:

- 2 cups raw almonds
- 1 tablespoon olive oil
- 1/2 teaspoon sea salt
- 1/2 teaspoon smoked paprika (optional)
- 1/4 teaspoon cayenne pepper (optional)

Instructions:

1. **Preheat the oven:** Preheat the oven to 350°F (175°C).
2. **Season the almonds:** Toss the almonds in olive oil, salt, paprika, and cayenne.
3. **Roast:** Spread the almonds on a baking sheet and roast for 10-15 minutes, stirring once or twice to ensure even roasting.
4. **Serve:** Let cool before serving.

Mini Sandwiches

Ingredients:

- 12 small rolls (slider buns)
- 1 lb deli meat (ham, turkey, or roast beef)
- 6 slices cheese (cheddar, Swiss, or provolone)
- 1/4 cup mayonnaise
- 1 tablespoon mustard
- Pickles, lettuce, and tomato (optional)

Instructions:

1. **Prepare the rolls:** Cut the slider buns in half.
2. **Assemble the sandwiches:** Spread mayonnaise and mustard on the buns. Layer with deli meat, cheese, and optional pickles, lettuce, and tomato.
3. **Serve:** Arrange the mini sandwiches on a platter and serve immediately.

Potato Wedges with Ketchup

Ingredients:

- 4 medium potatoes, cut into wedges
- 2 tablespoons olive oil
- 1 teaspoon garlic powder
- 1/2 teaspoon paprika
- Salt and pepper to taste
- Ketchup for dipping

Instructions:

1. **Preheat the oven:** Preheat the oven to 425°F (220°C).
2. **Prepare the potatoes:** Toss the potato wedges in olive oil, garlic powder, paprika, salt, and pepper.
3. **Roast:** Spread the wedges in a single layer on a baking sheet and bake for 25-30 minutes, flipping halfway through.
4. **Serve:** Serve hot with ketchup for dipping.

Baked Zucchini Fries

Ingredients:

- 2 medium zucchinis, cut into fries
- 1/2 cup breadcrumbs (preferably panko)
- 1/4 cup grated Parmesan cheese
- 1 teaspoon garlic powder
- 1/2 teaspoon paprika
- Salt and pepper to taste
- 1 egg, beaten

Instructions:

1. **Preheat the oven:** Preheat the oven to 400°F (200°C). Line a baking sheet with parchment paper.
2. **Prepare the zucchini:** Cut the zucchinis into fry-shaped strips.
3. **Coat the fries:** In a shallow bowl, mix the breadcrumbs, Parmesan cheese, garlic powder, paprika, salt, and pepper. Dip each zucchini fry into the beaten egg, then coat in the breadcrumb mixture.
4. **Bake:** Arrange the coated zucchini fries in a single layer on the baking sheet. Bake for 20-25 minutes, flipping halfway through, until golden and crispy.
5. **Serve:** Serve with marinara sauce or ranch dressing for dipping.

Chocolate Fudge Brownies

Ingredients:

- 1/2 cup unsalted butter, melted
- 1 cup granulated sugar
- 2 large eggs
- 1 teaspoon vanilla extract
- 1/3 cup unsweetened cocoa powder
- 1/2 cup all-purpose flour
- 1/4 teaspoon salt
- 1/4 teaspoon baking powder
- 1/2 cup chocolate chips (optional)

Instructions:

1. **Preheat the oven:** Preheat the oven to 350°F (175°C). Grease an 8x8-inch baking pan.
2. **Mix the wet ingredients:** In a large bowl, combine the melted butter, sugar, eggs, and vanilla extract.
3. **Add the dry ingredients:** Stir in the cocoa powder, flour, salt, and baking powder until well combined. Fold in chocolate chips if desired.
4. **Bake:** Pour the batter into the prepared baking pan. Bake for 20-25 minutes, or until a toothpick inserted into the center comes out with a few moist crumbs.
5. **Serve:** Let the brownies cool before cutting them into squares.

Cheese-Stuffed Mushrooms

Ingredients:

- 12 large mushrooms, stems removed
- 4 oz cream cheese, softened
- 1/4 cup grated Parmesan cheese
- 1/4 cup shredded mozzarella cheese
- 1 tablespoon garlic, minced
- 1/2 teaspoon dried thyme
- Salt and pepper to taste
- 1 tablespoon chopped parsley (for garnish)

Instructions:

1. **Preheat the oven:** Preheat the oven to 375°F (190°C).
2. **Prepare the mushrooms:** Remove the stems from the mushrooms and set the caps aside.
3. **Make the filling:** In a bowl, mix the cream cheese, Parmesan cheese, mozzarella cheese, garlic, thyme, salt, and pepper.
4. **Stuff the mushrooms:** Spoon the cheese mixture into each mushroom cap.
5. **Bake:** Arrange the stuffed mushrooms on a baking sheet and bake for 20 minutes, until the mushrooms are tender and the cheese is bubbly.
6. **Serve:** Garnish with chopped parsley before serving.

Rice Cake Crisps

Ingredients:

- 6 plain rice cakes, broken into pieces
- 2 tablespoons olive oil
- 1/2 teaspoon garlic powder
- 1/4 teaspoon paprika
- Salt and pepper to taste

Instructions:

1. **Preheat the oven:** Preheat the oven to 350°F (175°C). Line a baking sheet with parchment paper.
2. **Prepare the rice cakes:** Break the rice cakes into bite-sized pieces and place them on the baking sheet.
3. **Season:** Drizzle with olive oil and sprinkle with garlic powder, paprika, salt, and pepper.
4. **Bake:** Bake for 10-15 minutes, stirring halfway through, until crispy and golden.
5. **Serve:** Let cool and serve as a crunchy snack.

Chips and Salsa

Ingredients:

- 1 bag tortilla chips
- 2 cups diced tomatoes
- 1/2 cup red onion, finely chopped
- 1/4 cup cilantro, chopped
- 1 tablespoon lime juice
- Salt and pepper to taste

Instructions:

1. **Prepare the salsa:** In a bowl, combine the diced tomatoes, red onion, cilantro, lime juice, salt, and pepper.
2. **Serve:** Arrange the tortilla chips on a platter and serve with the fresh salsa.

Frozen Grapes

Ingredients:

- 2 cups grapes, washed and removed from stems
- 1 tablespoon honey (optional)

Instructions:

1. **Prepare the grapes:** Wash and remove the grapes from their stems. Pat dry with a paper towel.
2. **Freeze:** Place the grapes in a single layer on a baking sheet and freeze for 2-3 hours.
3. **Serve:** Once frozen, serve the grapes as a cool, refreshing snack. Drizzle with honey for added sweetness if desired.

Mini Burgers

Ingredients:

- 1 lb ground beef
- Salt and pepper to taste
- 12 small slider buns
- Cheese slices (optional)
- Lettuce, tomato, and pickles for garnish

Instructions:

1. **Make the patties:** Divide the ground beef into 12 small portions and shape each portion into a patty. Season with salt and pepper.
2. **Cook the burgers:** Heat a grill or skillet over medium-high heat. Cook the patties for 3-4 minutes per side, or until cooked to your desired level of doneness.
3. **Assemble the burgers:** Place the cooked patties on the slider buns and top with cheese, lettuce, tomato, and pickles.
4. **Serve:** Serve the mini burgers warm, with condiments on the side.

Chocolate-Covered Almonds

Ingredients:

- 1 cup raw almonds
- 1 cup dark chocolate chips
- 1 teaspoon coconut oil (optional)

Instructions:

1. **Toast the almonds:** Preheat the oven to 350°F (175°C). Spread the almonds in a single layer on a baking sheet and toast for 8-10 minutes, stirring halfway through.
2. **Melt the chocolate:** In a heatproof bowl, melt the dark chocolate chips and coconut oil (if using) over a double boiler or in the microwave.
3. **Coat the almonds:** Once the almonds are toasted and the chocolate is melted, dip each almond into the chocolate and place it on a parchment-lined baking sheet.
4. **Freeze:** Place the baking sheet in the freezer for 10-15 minutes to harden the chocolate.
5. **Serve:** Once the chocolate is set, serve the chocolate-covered almonds as a sweet snack.

Antipasto Skewers

Ingredients:

- 12 small wooden skewers
- 1/2 cup mozzarella balls
- 12 slices salami
- 12 cherry tomatoes
- 1/4 cup Kalamata olives
- 12 small basil leaves
- 1/4 cup marinated artichoke hearts, drained and halved
- Olive oil, for drizzling
- Balsamic glaze (optional)

Instructions:

1. **Assemble the skewers:** Thread the ingredients onto each skewer, starting with a cherry tomato, followed by a mozzarella ball, a slice of salami, an olive, a basil leaf, and an artichoke heart.
2. **Serve:** Arrange the skewers on a platter. Drizzle with olive oil and balsamic glaze before serving for added flavor.

Spinach and Artichoke Dip

Ingredients:

- 1 cup frozen spinach, thawed and drained
- 1 cup marinated artichoke hearts, chopped
- 1 cup cream cheese, softened
- 1/2 cup sour cream
- 1/2 cup mayonnaise
- 1 cup shredded mozzarella cheese
- 1/2 cup grated Parmesan cheese
- 1 teaspoon garlic powder
- Salt and pepper to taste

Instructions:

1. **Prepare the dip:** In a large bowl, combine the spinach, artichokes, cream cheese, sour cream, mayonnaise, mozzarella, Parmesan, garlic powder, salt, and pepper.
2. **Bake:** Preheat the oven to 375°F (190°C). Transfer the dip mixture into a baking dish and bake for 20-25 minutes, until the top is golden and bubbly.
3. **Serve:** Serve the dip warm with tortilla chips, pita bread, or fresh veggies for dipping.

Mini Quiches

Ingredients:

- 1 pre-made pie crust, cut into small circles (or use mini tart shells)
- 4 large eggs
- 1/2 cup milk or heavy cream
- 1/2 cup shredded cheese (cheddar, Swiss, or your choice)
- 1/4 cup cooked spinach, chopped
- 1/4 cup cooked bacon or sausage (optional)
- Salt and pepper to taste

Instructions:

1. **Prepare the filling:** In a bowl, whisk together the eggs, milk, cheese, spinach, bacon or sausage (if using), salt, and pepper.
2. **Assemble the quiches:** Place the mini pie crusts or tart shells on a baking sheet. Pour the egg mixture into each shell, filling them about 3/4 full.
3. **Bake:** Preheat the oven to 350°F (175°C). Bake for 12-15 minutes, or until the quiches are set and lightly browned on top.
4. **Serve:** Let cool slightly before serving as a bite-sized snack.

Caramel Popcorn

Ingredients:

- 10 cups popped popcorn (about 1/2 cup unpopped kernels)
- 1 cup unsalted butter
- 1 cup brown sugar, packed
- 1/2 cup light corn syrup
- 1 teaspoon vanilla extract
- 1/2 teaspoon baking soda
- 1/4 teaspoon salt

Instructions:

1. **Preheat the oven:** Preheat the oven to 250°F (120°C). Line a large baking sheet with parchment paper.
2. **Make the caramel:** In a saucepan, melt the butter over medium heat. Stir in the brown sugar, corn syrup, and salt. Bring to a boil while stirring frequently. Once it starts boiling, let it cook for 4-5 minutes without stirring.
3. **Coat the popcorn:** Remove the caramel from the heat and stir in the vanilla extract and baking soda. Pour the caramel sauce over the popped popcorn and toss to coat evenly.
4. **Bake:** Spread the caramel-coated popcorn onto the prepared baking sheet. Bake for 45 minutes, stirring every 15 minutes to ensure even coating.
5. **Serve:** Let the caramel popcorn cool before serving. Store in an airtight container.

Dried Fruit Mix

Ingredients:

- 1/2 cup dried cranberries
- 1/2 cup dried apricots, chopped
- 1/2 cup raisins
- 1/2 cup dried mango, chopped
- 1/4 cup dried pineapple, chopped
- 1/4 cup almonds or cashews (optional)

Instructions:

1. **Combine the fruit:** In a bowl, mix together all the dried fruits and nuts (if using).
2. **Serve:** Serve immediately or store in an airtight container for later. This mix is great as a snack on its own or added to yogurt or cereal.

Onion Rings

Ingredients:

- 2 large onions, sliced into rings
- 1 cup buttermilk
- 1 cup all-purpose flour
- 1 teaspoon garlic powder
- 1/2 teaspoon paprika
- Salt and pepper to taste
- Vegetable oil for frying

Instructions:

1. **Soak the onions:** Place the onion rings in a bowl and cover with buttermilk. Let them soak for 30 minutes.
2. **Prepare the batter:** In a separate bowl, mix the flour, garlic powder, paprika, salt, and pepper.
3. **Coat the onions:** Heat the vegetable oil in a large pot or deep fryer over medium heat. Dip each onion ring into the flour mixture, ensuring it's evenly coated, and then fry in batches for 2-3 minutes or until golden and crispy.
4. **Serve:** Drain the onion rings on paper towels and serve hot with your favorite dipping sauce.

Popcorn Chicken

Ingredients:

- 1 lb chicken breast, cut into small bite-sized pieces
- 1 cup buttermilk
- 1 cup all-purpose flour
- 1/2 teaspoon garlic powder
- 1/2 teaspoon onion powder
- 1/2 teaspoon paprika
- Salt and pepper to taste
- Vegetable oil for frying

Instructions:

1. **Marinate the chicken:** Place the chicken pieces in a bowl and cover with buttermilk. Let them marinate for at least 30 minutes.
2. **Prepare the coating:** In a shallow bowl, combine the flour, garlic powder, onion powder, paprika, salt, and pepper.
3. **Coat the chicken:** Heat the vegetable oil in a large pan or deep fryer over medium-high heat. Coat each piece of chicken with the seasoned flour mixture, pressing gently to adhere.
4. **Fry the chicken:** Fry the chicken in batches for 3-4 minutes, or until golden brown and cooked through.
5. **Serve:** Drain the chicken on paper towels and serve with dipping sauces like honey mustard or ranch.

Parmesan Crisps

Ingredients:

- 1 1/2 cups shredded Parmesan cheese
- Freshly ground black pepper (optional)
- Fresh herbs (optional)

Instructions:

1. **Preheat the oven:** Preheat the oven to 400°F (200°C). Line a baking sheet with parchment paper.
2. **Make the crisps:** Scoop 1 tablespoon of Parmesan cheese and form small mounds on the baking sheet, spacing them a few inches apart. Press lightly to flatten each mound.
3. **Bake:** Bake for 5-7 minutes, or until golden and crispy. Keep an eye on them to prevent burning.
4. **Serve:** Let cool on the baking sheet for a minute before transferring to a plate. Serve as a snack or with your favorite dip. Optionally, season with freshly ground black pepper or herbs like rosemary or thyme for extra flavor.

Chocolate-Covered Strawberries

Ingredients:

- 1 lb fresh strawberries, washed and dried
- 8 oz dark chocolate (or milk chocolate), chopped
- 4 oz white chocolate, chopped (optional, for drizzling)

Instructions:

1. **Melt the chocolate:** Place the dark chocolate in a heatproof bowl over a pot of simmering water (double boiler method), stirring until smooth and melted.
2. **Dip the strawberries:** Hold each strawberry by the stem and dip it into the melted dark chocolate, coating it halfway. Let any excess chocolate drip off.
3. **Optional white chocolate drizzle:** Melt the white chocolate in a separate bowl and drizzle over the dipped strawberries for a decorative touch.
4. **Cool:** Place the dipped strawberries on a parchment-lined tray and refrigerate for about 30 minutes to allow the chocolate to set.
5. **Serve:** Once the chocolate has hardened, serve the strawberries chilled.

Sausage Rolls

Ingredients:

- 1 lb sausage meat (or ground sausage)
- 1 sheet puff pastry (thawed if frozen)
- 1 egg (beaten, for egg wash)
- 1 teaspoon dried thyme (optional)

Instructions:

1. **Prepare the sausage filling:** If using sausage links, remove the casing and crumble the sausage. Optionally, add thyme for extra flavor.
2. **Assemble the rolls:** Roll out the puff pastry on a floured surface. Spread the sausage mixture evenly along one edge of the pastry. Roll the pastry over the sausage to form a log, then cut into bite-sized pieces.
3. **Egg wash:** Brush the tops of the rolls with the beaten egg to help them brown.
4. **Bake:** Preheat the oven to 400°F (200°C). Place the sausage rolls on a baking sheet and bake for 15-20 minutes, or until golden brown and crispy.
5. **Serve:** Serve hot, with mustard or ketchup for dipping.

Veggie and Cheese Kabobs

Ingredients:

- 1 cup cherry tomatoes
- 1 cucumber, sliced
- 1 bell pepper, cut into chunks
- 1 small red onion, cut into chunks
- 1 block of cheese (cheddar, mozzarella, or your choice), cut into cubes
- Fresh basil leaves (optional)
- Olive oil and balsamic vinegar (for drizzling)

Instructions:

1. **Prepare the vegetables:** Cut the vegetables and cheese into bite-sized pieces.
2. **Assemble the kabobs:** On small skewers or toothpicks, alternate threading the cherry tomatoes, cucumber, bell pepper, red onion, cheese cubes, and basil leaves if using.
3. **Serve:** Arrange the kabobs on a platter. Drizzle with olive oil and balsamic vinegar just before serving for extra flavor.

Cinnamon Apple Chips

Ingredients:

- 2 apples, thinly sliced (use a mandoline if possible)
- 1/2 teaspoon cinnamon
- 1 tablespoon sugar (optional)

Instructions:

1. **Preheat the oven:** Preheat the oven to 225°F (110°C). Line a baking sheet with parchment paper.
2. **Prepare the apples:** Core and slice the apples very thinly. Lay the slices out on the prepared baking sheet in a single layer.
3. **Season:** Sprinkle the apple slices with cinnamon and sugar (if using).
4. **Bake:** Bake for 1-2 hours, turning the apples halfway through, until they are crispy and golden.
5. **Serve:** Let cool before serving. Store in an airtight container for up to a week.

Baked Brie with Crackers

Ingredients:

- 1 wheel of Brie cheese
- 2 tablespoons honey or jam (optional)
- Fresh herbs like thyme (optional)
- Crackers, for serving

Instructions:

1. **Preheat the oven:** Preheat the oven to 350°F (175°C).
2. **Bake the Brie:** Place the wheel of Brie on a baking dish and bake for 10-12 minutes, or until the cheese is soft and melted inside.
3. **Serve:** Drizzle with honey or your favorite jam and sprinkle with fresh herbs if desired. Serve with crackers or sliced baguette.

Puffed Rice Bars

Ingredients:

- 3 cups puffed rice cereal
- 1/2 cup peanut butter (or almond butter)
- 1/4 cup honey
- 1/2 teaspoon vanilla extract
- 1/4 cup chocolate chips (optional)

Instructions:

1. **Prepare the mixture:** In a saucepan, heat the peanut butter and honey over medium heat until melted and smooth. Stir in vanilla extract.
2. **Combine:** Pour the puffed rice into a large bowl and pour the peanut butter mixture over it. Stir to coat evenly.
3. **Set the bars:** Press the mixture into a greased 9x9-inch baking pan and let cool for about 30 minutes.
4. **Optional chocolate topping:** If using chocolate chips, melt them and drizzle over the cooled bars.
5. **Serve:** Cut into bars and enjoy.

Mini Pancakes with Syrup

Ingredients:

- 1 cup pancake mix
- 1/2 cup milk
- 1 egg
- 1 tablespoon melted butter
- Maple syrup, for serving

Instructions:

1. **Prepare the batter:** In a bowl, whisk together the pancake mix, milk, egg, and melted butter until smooth.
2. **Cook the pancakes:** Heat a griddle or nonstick skillet over medium heat. Spoon small amounts of batter to form mini pancakes. Cook for 1-2 minutes on each side, or until golden brown.
3. **Serve:** Stack the mini pancakes and serve with maple syrup for dipping.

www.ingramcontent.com/pod-product-compliance
Lightning Source LLC
LaVergne TN
LVHW081504060526
838201LV00056BA/2918